Skylarks and Seagulls

Children of Portlethen

Elizabeth A Dodds

Published in 2015
with the help of Lumphanan Press
Roddenbrae, Lumphanan
Aberdeenshire, AB31 4RN

www.lumphananpress.co.uk

Printed and bound by Imprint Digital,
Upton Pyne, Devon, UK

ISBN: 978-0-9927468-3-4

Contents

For Stuart, Marilyn and Sandra,
and in memory of our parents.

Introduction

In 1939 my parents, Alexander Dunn from Beith in Ayrshire and Florence Hourston from Evie in Orkney, married and came to live in Portlethen. My father had just been appointed minister of Portlethen Church and so they moved into The Manse, a big stone house with a walled garden, surrounded by woodland and open fields. In 1941, my brother, Stuart was born there. I followed in 1942, my sister, Marilyn, in 1944 and Sandra in 1947.

As children, Portlethen was our world. We went to school in the Primary School, bought sweets in Mrs Thompson's shop, posted letters at Miss Chalmer's Post Office. We went to Sunday School in the Church on top of the hill and to concerts and Christmas parties in the Jubilee Hall. We helped our parents cut peat in the Moss and went tattie picking on the farms with all the other school children. The countryside around Portlethen was our playground. We climbed trees in the Manse Wood, paddled in the burn, made dens in the drystane dykes and in the stooks at harvestime. We ran across the Moss and scrambled up and down the cliffs at the shore with the freedom allowed children in these days.

At that time, Portlethen was a community of mainly farmers and fishermen, with some residents commuting daily into Aberdeen to work, living in houses clustered round the station, school and church. During the war, there was a group of service personnel living on the RAF station next to the Craighead stone circle and, after the war, people who had been bombed out of Aberdeen were housed in a temporary camp near Adam's Smiddy. During all the years we lived in Portlethen, very little changed. As a young child, I used to go with my father to visit Mr Adam, the blacksmith, and watch the big cart horses being brought in from the farms to be shod, but it was not long before the horses disappeared from the fields and only tractors were seen pulling the ploughs. As school children we watched the radar pylons being demolished and the houses at Burnside Gardens built, and in 1955 when the station closed we had to get used to travelling to Mackie Academy in Stonehaven by bus instead of train. Otherwise our lives followed a constant pattern, season after season, year after year.

The stories in this book give a view of life in Portlethen at that time before the coming of the oil industry, seen through the eyes of the children in one family. I have written them for my brother and sisters but also for all the people who live in Portlethen now and are interested in learning something of the history of this very special place.

Elizabeth Dodds (nee Dunn)
9th July, 2015

Acknowledgements

These stories are a record of my own memories together with those of my brother and sisters and I want to thank Stuart Dunn, Marilyn Stronach and Sandra Edwards for their contributions.

I also want to thank the members of the Beeston Writing Group and particularly my first tutor, Mike Wareham, for encouraging me to start writing down some of my memories of a childhood in a place so far away from Nottingham where I live now.

I am grateful to Allan Dodds and Fraser Stronach for their help with the photographs and to John Edwards for his many practical suggestions.

I want to thank Allan Dodds for giving me permission to reproduce the oil painting depicted on the cover: Edwin J Smith painted "Figures on a Beach" in 1916.

My thanks also go to friends, particularly Jean, Susan, Margaret, Judith, Trish, Elvire and Christine for their constant support and encouragement, and to my family here in England, Allan, Jenny and Jonathan.

A very special thank you goes to my grandchildren, Ellen and James, who used to say, "Granny, tell me a story about when you were a little girl"

January

Portlethen on a snowy day –
view from the church war memorial.

Snowed In

We wake up, jump out of our beds, pull open the curtains and find that overnight our world has turned white. We stand, barefooted, at the window and watch the snowflakes falling, quietly, slowly, down, down, swirling, spiralling, floating like ash on the still air, burying the garden till only the dark tops of the blackcurrant bushes stand out like islands in the sea of white. We watch the snow settling on the roof of the barn, balancing on top of the garden wall, shrouding the cheese press in the corner of the courtyard, covering everything in a cold white blanket. We see the snow lying along the branches of the trees in the Manse Wood till they look like silvery fingers spread out against a dark grey sky, and beyond them the patchwork of snow covered fields rising to the distant hills.

I pull open the sash window, shivering in the draught of icy air. Marilyn stretches out her hand to catch a snowflake and we watch as it melts and disappears. How quiet everything is – no clucking hens scratching around the courtyard, no hum of cars and lorries on the Aberdeen road. The world is silent, still.

"Breakfast time, children," shouts Mum from the foot of the stairs.

We slam the window shut, shrug our arms into knitted jerseys, pull on our dungarees and woollen socks and race downstairs. The kitchen is warm with peat burning in the cast iron stove. Dad and Stuart are already sitting at the table tucking into plates of porridge and milk. Mum is coaxing our little sister, Sandra, to eat up her poached egg on toast.

"It looks like it's been snowing all night," says Dad.

Mum looks anxiously at the snowflakes tumbling past the kitchen window.

"I'll need to get out to the barn to feed the hens and collect the eggs," she says.

Dad finishes his breakfast, gets up from the table, and opens the back door.

"Goodness me," he says, "It's more than three feet deep out here."

He comes back into the kitchen, fetches his wellington boots from the cupboard under the stairs, picks up a shovel from beside the stove and goes outside to start digging us out. He cuts and lifts and throws the snow, slowly, steadily, scooping out a path towards the courtyard. We gulp down our breakfast, grab our coats and boots and go to help him.

"Stuart, can you dig a path to the peat shed and take a bucket of peat in to your Mum?" says Dad.

"Girls, see if you can reach the barn door and then fetch a

basket and collect the eggs."

Me and Marilyn fetch a spade and a brush from the tool shed and dig a path to the barn, push the door open and squeeze inside. We wrinkle up our noses at the musty smell from the peat litter and turn to meet the pink-eyed stare of a hundred White Leghorns perched on their roosts.

"Sorry, hens," I say. "You can't go out today. It's too cold and snowy, but, cheer up, your breakfast's coming in a minute. Now, have you got any eggs for us this morning?"

The hens reply with a chorus of contented clucks. I hold the ladder and Marilyn climbs up to the nest boxes and hands me the warm, newly laid eggs. We fill the basket and carry it carefully into the kitchen. We hurry back outside.

By now the courtyard is criss-crossed with steep–sided tunnels cut into a wall of snow. We see a red woolly hat bobbing up and down and hear the sound of a dog barking and know that Sandra and our little Shetland collie, Magnus, are having fun running along the paths. We follow the sound of voices out to the Manse Road where Dad and Stuart are standing chatting to Mr Milne from Gushetneuk.

"Do you notice that there's no cars running on the main road?" says Mr Milne. "I heard on the phone this morning that the snow plough set off from Aberdeen but ran into the back of a single decker bus that was half-buried in a snow drift."

"They'll start by trying to get the traffic moving on the main road," says Dad. "It'll be a while before they get round to clearing the road down to Portlethen. So it looks like we'll be snowed in for a day or two."

Dad and Mr Milne look serious but we think it sounds rather

exciting. At that moment, down the road come Kathleen and Sandy Milne dragging their sledge.

"We're going sledging on the Post Office brae," they shout. "Are you coming?"

We skip off to fetch our sledges from the garage and follow Kathleen and Sandy down the Manse Road to the hill that runs past the Post Office. Stuart grabs the back of his sledge, runs as fast as he can then launches himself stomach first onto his sledge, using his feet hanging out behind him to steer himself away from the ditches and walls on either side of the road. Kathleen and Sandy go next. Now it's our turn. Marilyn sits on at the front, Sandra on her knee. I push as hard as I can till we pick up speed, then jump on behind them and down we whizz, gathering speed on the slope, faster and faster, till finally we glide to a stop by the bridge over the burn. We drag the sledge up the hill and off we go again. This time Sandra lies on Stuart's back and goes down the hill with him. On the next run Marilyn and I forget to steer and end up in a snowdrift at the side of the road. As the morning wears on, other children from houses nearby join us till there's about twenty of us, shouting, laughing, sliding, hurtling up and down the hill. There's no traffic to worry about. For this day, the road belongs to us children.

Around midday we hear a distant "Cooee." It's Mum calling us home for dinner. We trudge up the Manse Road, Stuart pulling Sandra on his sledge, in through the back gate and follow the path to the door. We leave our boots in the scullery and sit down at the kitchen table for a big plate of mince and tatties. We tell Mum all about the sledging but we can see she's only half-listening. She's worrying about how we're going to manage now we're snowed in.

"We're running out of milk. How're we going to fetch it from the farm?" she says.

"Don't worry," says Stuart, "I have a plan."

After dinner, Stuart calls our little dog, Magnus, and disappears out to the garage. He reappears moments later with Magnus in a harness attached to a sledge.

"You can't do that," says Marilyn. "He's too little to pull a sledge."

"Don't worry," says Stuart. "Look, I have a rope. I'm pulling too," and off they go, the pair of them, up the Manse Road towards Balquharn. An hour later they're back carrying three pails of milk balanced on the sledge, one for the Milnes, one for Miss Chalmers at the Post Office, and one for us. Magnus is barking with excitement and none the worse for his spell as a sledge dog. We give him a cuddle and tell him what a clever dog he is.

As the winter sun falls toward the hills in the west, we roll a big snowball on the front lawn and turn it into a snowman. We give him eyes made from lumps of coal, a carrot for a nose and dress him in one of Dad's old coats. When darkness falls, we drift back into the warmth of the kitchen. Dad has gone out visiting round his parish, but soon comes in the door saying, "I was coming down the path toward the front door and suddenly there was a strange man wearing a long dark coat, standing in the middle of the lawn, glaring at me with big black eyes. I got such a fright that I turned and ran for my life."

We laugh and tell him what a good day we've had. We know it's a nuisance that he can't get his car out of the garage, that Mum has to worry about bread and milk running out but we like being snowed in.

February

Elizabeth Dunn, Sandy Milne, Rhoda Duncan, Linda McKay, Miss Jenkins our teacher and Kathleen Milne – sitting on the bank outside the Manse garden gate, in front of the Scots pine tree which was blown down in the 1953 gales.

The Great Storm

We wake, me and Marilyn, to the sound of the wind. We lie, cosy and warm, in our bed tucked under the eaves in the attic and listen. Sometimes we hear an eerie moaning like someone in pain, searching for a way in through chinks in the stonewalls or down the chimney, looking for comfort. Sometimes there is a scream of rage and we hear the wind shouting at the house,

"How dare you stand in my path? Get out of my way or I'll flatten you."

We hear the windows rattling as if someone big and fierce is crawling over the slate roof and is trying to get in and grab us. We're frightened and pull the quilt up over our heads.

Then comes the sound of footsteps on the stairs and we pop our heads out from under the covers just as the bedroom door opens and there is Mum, smiling.

"Time to get up, girls. Put on your warm clothes – it's a very windy day."

We hop out of bed. If Mum thinks it's just "a very windy day" then there's nothing to worry about.

We get dressed quickly, clatter down the stairs. The fire is lit in the range and the kitchen is warm. Stuart and Sandra are sitting at the table eating their porridge. Dad switches on the radio and listens to the news. We hear the newsreader saying that there's gale force winds blowing, that there's trees down all over Scotland and that the wind has caused a storm surge and blown the waves over the seawalls, flooding lots of low lying land, but far away down south in England, not here. We're perched on top of cliffs, hundreds of feet high up in the air, so the sea can't reach us.

After breakfast we go upstairs to look out the window in the front bedroom. We can see the sky, grey and sullen, scowling down at us, dark clouds hurtling overhead. We watch the ash tree at the corner of the garden lurch and sway like a drunken old man, knarled hands twisting and squirming, tips snapping off and falling to the ground. We hear in the distance a crash of branches and an echoing thud.

"That's a tree falling down in the wood," says Stuart. He pauses for a moment. "What if the ash tree falls down? It'll land on the house. It'll come through my bedroom ceiling. It'll squash us all standing here."

We stare out the window in horror. Which way is the wind blowing? Will the tree fall towards us or away from us? We can't tell. The wind seems to be swirling in all directions. Suddenly there is a crack and a rumble and we watch as the garden wall next to the ash tree splits and crumbles, stones and rubble tumbling down the bank into the field.

"The tree's loosening its roots," says Stuart. "It's going to fall down."

We turn and flee down the stairs to the kitchen at the back of the house where the tree can't get to us. Mum is there talking to Dad.

"What about the hens? I'll need to go and feed them," says Mum.

"Bit of a problem," says Dad. "I've been watching out the window and there's slates flying off the roof. Hmm! Let me think," and off he goes into the cupboard under the stairs and reappears with the army hard hat that belonged to his father when he was fighting in the First World War.

Mum shrugs her arms into her coat, ties the belt tightly and claps the army hat on her head. She opens the back door letting in a gust of wind that scatters the newspapers by the fireside. She bangs the door shut behind her. We all rush upstairs to the back bedroom to watch as she crosses the courtyard, head down, coat flapping, buffeted by the gale. How brave she is! She disappears into the peat shed, comes out with a pail of corn and goes into the barn where the hens live. We wait anxiously for her to reappear and battle her way back home. We run down to the kitchen to give her a hug and help her off with her coat. Everyone wants to try on the old army hat.

We spend the rest of the day listening to the radio, playing dominos and cards round the kitchen table but as night falls the wind dies down and we're able to venture outside. We see the lawn littered with broken branches and twigs, with fallen roof slates tangled among the rose bushes.

"Come and see," says Dad and we follow him along the path to the front garden gate. What a surprise! We can't get out to the Manse Road because, blocking the way, is the trunk of the Scots Pine tree that has always stood on the bank just outside the gate. All our life we've played hide and seek round this tree, we've gathered pine cones under it, we've had our photograph taken in front of it. It has always been there, tall and strong, guarding the entrance to the Manse. Now we can see it lying flat with its head buried in the snowberry bushes and its roots sticking up in the air, broken, bare-earthed.

As we stand quietly, remembering, out of the gloom comes Mr Milne from up the road.

"How're you all doing? Survived the storm?" he says. "It looks like you could do with a bit of a hand. I'll be down in the morning with my saw and we'll cut a path out for you."

At bedtime, we sit round the kitchen table drinking our cocoa, talking over everything that has happened. We've lost the Scots Pine, a bit of the garden wall, some slates off the roof but the ash tree didn't fall down on the house, the hens got fed and Mr Milne's coming in the morning with his saw to help cut a path out to the road. We've survived the Great Storm.

March

Rev Alexander Dunn conducting
a wedding service in Portlethen church

The Church Mouse

It's Sunday morning and dressed in our best clothes, we file into the Manse pew in Portlethen Church. Stuart sprawls next to the side aisle, and beside him sits Mum in her fur coat and her navy felt hat, worrying away about the roast chicken left in the oven back home. Snuggled into Mum's fur coat is little sister, Sandra, and beside her is Marilyn, two years younger than me, fair curly hair, big blue eyes, good as gold, never in trouble, not like me. I sit farthest away from Mum, in my tweed coat with the velvet collar and my brown bowler hat, propping up my hymnbook on the ledge in front ready for the singing. I shake off my shoes and wrap my stockinged feet round the hot pipe that runs under the footrest.

Next to me in the pew sit the Craig family, Mr Andrew Craig and his two sisters, all totally blind. Every Sunday morning we stand outside by the War Memorial waiting for the service to start and watch the Craigs walk up the road from the

Portlethen Village, arms linked, Mr Craig tapping ahead of them with his white stick. I've no idea how they know when they've reached the foot of the church brae but they make their way up the hill and into church without ever bumping into anything. They know all the words of the hymns and sing along with us without reading the hymnbook.

I look around the church. Miss Richmond, the organist, is pedalling away furiously on the old organ, rocking from side to side, playing a bit of Handel while people take their seats. I see Lillian and Eileen Milne, my friend Kathleen's big sisters, sitting in the front row of the choir. They're looking very smartly dressed as usual, bright red lipstick, hats at a jaunty angle. I see the communion table with the brass vase full of orange and yellow daffodils, picked from the Manse garden this morning. I see the stained glass window with it's saints in bright blue and green robes and the picture in the corner of seagulls flying over a fishing trawler, supposed to represent the fishermen of Portlethen, though all I've ever seen down at the shore are the salmon cobble and a few small boats stacked with creels for catching lobsters.

I look up at the three-masted sailing ship that hangs from the ceiling and wonder how they managed to fix it up there. What if the string that holds it in place breaks? That would be a surprise, especially if you were directly underneath when it fell.

The door to the vestry opens and in comes Maxie Gray, the beadle, carrying the black leather Bible. He climbs the pulpit steps, sets the Bible on the lectern, and comes back down and stands like a sentry at the foot of the steps. Then in comes Dad, dressed in his black gown with the red hood, head bowed over the papers in his hand. He looks very solemn – very different from the Dad who laughs his head off over Oor Willie and the Broons in the Sunday Post. He goes up the pulpit steps and sits down.

The service starts. Hymn, prayer, hymn, reading, hymn, prayer. We stand up, sit down, stand up, sit down again. Then it's time for the sermon. This is my cue to get out the Sunday School magazine. I read the stories about missionaries doing good deeds in Africa. I take a pencil from my pocket and do the Bible crossword – easy if you've been to church and Sunday School every week since you were 5 years old. Dad's busy with his tripartite sermon – firstly, secondly, not yet reached thirdly and finally, so I know there's at least ten minutes to go before he's finished.

What will I do now? I know. I'll make a mouse with my handkerchief. I get my cotton handkerchief out of my coat pocket and fold it diagonally into a triangle. I roll up each corner towards the middle. I'm aware Marilyn has stopped reading her magazine and is watching with interest. I fold the rolled handkerchief over, tuck in the ends, and then unroll it to form the body of the mouse. I pull out one corner. Good, that's the tail. I pull out the other corner, tie it in a knot to make the head and two ears. Perfect!

I hold my little mouse in the palm of my hand and stroke it slowly, gently. Marilyn watches. Slowly, gently, stroke, stroke. Suddenly, I twitch my fingers and the mouse shoots up my arm. Marilyn starts to laugh. I can see Mum leaning forward and frowning. I sit back, hidden by my two sisters, and hold the mouse in the palm of my hand again. Stroke, stroke, slowly, quietly, then a quick twitch and it shoots up my arm and over my shoulder. Marilyn is in hysterics, covering her mouth with her hand to muffle the giggles. Mum leans forward and gives Marilyn a little tap on the knee.

"Sh! Behave yourself," whispers Mum. Amazing! Marilyn, who never does anything wrong, is getting the blame. But then I look up and see Dad looking sternly at me from the pulpit. Oh dear, I'm in trouble. Better behave or he'll bring the wrath of God down on me and I'll be turned into a pillar of salt like Lot's wife or eaten alive by a plague of locusts like the Egyptians.

I retrieve the mouse from my shoulder and put it in my pocket. Dad is starting The Lord's Prayer and we all join in.

"Lead us not into temptation and deliver us from evil."

I will try.

April

Portlethen Shore with the bothy for the salmon fishermen,
wooden runners down to the sea for the cobble and posts
for drying the nets.

Portlethen Shore

It's a sunny afternoon in the school holidays and we decide to abandon our usual playground in the fields and woods around The Manse and go on an expedition to Portlethen shore. There's five of us, me, my brother, Stuart, Kathleen and Sandy Milne, the twins from up the road and Sandy Moir from Cookston Cottages. We run and skip along the road, chasing each other, shouting, and laughing. We pass the school and the village hall, round the corner past Mrs Thompson's shop and over the railway bridge. We hear the sound of a train coming and lean over the wall to watch the steam engine, dragging its fleet of wagons, puffing along the track from Aberdeen. We wait till we're buried in smoke as it passes under the bridge then run across to the other side to watch it reappear and chug its way south to Stonehaven. We hurry on along the road, past the church up on the hill, then on past the farmyard, the byres and barns of The Mains of Portlethen.

We stop for a moment to watch the black and white cows with their calves, then we're onto the narrow grassy track sheltered between high, stone walls which takes us down to the top of the cliffs.

We pause to catch our breath and look around us. The cliffs are awash with wild flowers – purple heather, blue harebells and pale cream primroses. Below us the waves crash and thunder against the rocks, and we hear the granite boulders grinding against each other as the current sweeps in and out. Offshore the island of May Craig is alive with gulls, wheeling and circling overhead, crying out to each other. The smell of seaweed hangs in the salty air.

Then we're running, helter-skelter down the fern-lined path, past the war-time, concrete anti-tank blocks, past the fishermen's bothy, dancing sure-footedly over the boulders down to the water's edge. Me and Kathleen find a seat on the wooden runners used to winch the salmon cobble on to the beach and take off our socks and shoes. We step gingerly along the planks, green and slippery with algae and dip our toes in the icy North Sea. Stuart and the other lads are picking up flat stones then, with a flick of the wrist, sending them skipping and dancing over the surface of the sea. Me and Kathleen dry our feet on our cardigans, wriggle our damp toes into our socks and shoes and go exploring among the rocks at the foot of the cliffs. We find a pool, marooned by the ebbing tide, and lie down to dangle our hands in the still water trying to catch the tiny crabs and fish which swim among the brown and green seaweed.

We hear shouts and laughter and stand up to investigate.

We can see Stuart and his friends have started a new game. They are standing on a big rock, waiting till a wave washes in and out then jumping onto a small rock and quickly off again onto the rocks at the other side of the deep-water channel, shouting with excitement as they dodge the incoming wave. Me and Kathleen stand and watch. Looks like fun. Will we give it a go? Anything boys can do, girls can do just as well.

We hop down off our rocky perch and go to join the lads. I'm in the queue behind Stuart, and Sandy Milne is behind me. Stuart jumps onto the rock and off again. Looks easy. Now it's my turn. I wait till a wave has ebbed out then jump. I struggle to keep my balance on the slippery rock and hesitate. Behind me there's a shout from Sandy then his body crashes into mine sending me flying. I'm falling, down into the shockingly cold sea. A wave crashes over me, deafening me, blinding me. I am rolling and banging against rocks. Salt water gets in my eyes and up my nose. I can't see. I can't breathe. I struggle to get to my feet but the current sweeps my legs out from under me. I am panic-stricken, terrified. Suddenly a hand grabs the back of my cardigan and I'm dragged upright. I feel Stuart's arm round my shoulders steadying me as I stumble over rocks and pebbles out of the sea onto the beach. I sit on a rock coughing and spluttering.

"I thought she was going to jump," mutters Sandy. The others look on in silence.

"We'll need to go home," says Stuart and one after the other we make our way slowly up the path to the cliff top and trudge, quiet and subdued, along the road past the farm, past the church, over the railway bridge. I am soaked through, my long hair hanging like rats' tails around my face, shoes squelching as I walk. I am shivering, half with cold, half with shock, biting my lip to stop myself crying. We plod on past the shop. I keep my head down so that I can't see people staring at me. At the Post Office, Sandy Moir mutters his goodbye and heads off for his house. We leave the twins at the back gate and me and Stuart make our way into the house.

Mum is in the kitchen baking scones with our little sisters. She looks up as we come in.

"Elizabeth fell in the sea," says Stuart.

I burst into tears and stand sobbing and shivering. Mum lays down her wooden spoon, takes my hand and leads me through to the bathroom and shuts the door. She puts the plug in the bath and turns on the taps. She strips off my wet clothes and lifts me into the warm water. Gently she bathes my bruised elbows and scratched knees, murmuring words of comfort and reassurance. She washes my hair and I lie down and let the warm soapy water carry away the memory of the cold salty sea. Mum lifts me out, wraps me in a warm towel and holds me close. I feel safe again.

May

The Dunn Family: Elizabeth, Sandra, Rev Alexander Dunn,
Mrs Florence Dunn, Marilyn and Stuart

Big Night Out

It's Friday night and we're home from school. Mum has our tea waiting. We dump the school bags, wash hands and face, have a quick gulp of something to eat, grab the music books and pile into the Dad's car, Stuart in the front seat, me, Marilyn and Sandra squashed in the back of the Ford Anglia.

Then we're bumping down the ruts and puddles of the Manse Road, up to the crossroads at Adam's Smiddy and turning out onto the Aberdeen road. We drive along past Hillside and Findon, past the fork in the road at the Loch of Lauriston, over the hill until, suddenly, there below us is the River Dee, winding its way seaward from the Grampians, and slate-roofed, granite-walled Aberdeen. It's down the hill past Kincorth, across the narrow Bridge of Dee, up Holburn Street to Forest Avenue.

Stuart and I jump out, knock on Mr Center's door, and in we go for our music lessons. Marilyn and Sandra head for

Miss Law and her piano a few streets away. Then it's scales, arpeggios, flats, sharps, andante, pianissimo, Beethoven and Mozart for an hour until finally we're free and out we go to find Dad waiting patiently in the front seat of the car, reading his "World's Fair" which he collects from the paper shop in Belmont Street. Dad grew up in Beith in Ayrshire which holds an annual Beith Fair. Over the years he got to know lots of people who travel with fairs and circuses and likes to keep up with their news. We open the car door and climb in. Dad folds his paper and switches on the car engine.

We drive to Miss Law's and pick up Marilyn and Sandra, and then we're off again along Union Street, turning left into Diamond Street, parking outside the News Cinema. In we go and Dad goes to the kiosk to buy the tickets – one adult, four children. We follow the usherette with her torch into the dark of the cinema and settle ourselves in our seats. Pathe News is on and a man with a polite English accent is telling us what's going on in the world while the cine projector whirrs and sends its beam of light out of the darkness on to the screen. There are stories of earthquakes and floods, of weddings and funerals, of conflicts and revolutions, of cricket and football matches – so many different countries, so many interesting people, so many exciting things happening in the world far away from Aberdeen. Then it's cartoon time and we all laugh but we keep an eye on Dad because sometimes he laughs so much he gets hiccups. After an hour of magic, the programme is finished and out we file into the evening light.

Next stop is the fish and chip shop in Holburn Street and it's a threepenny poke of chips for each of us and a competition to see who can make theirs last longest.

"Where to now?" asks Dad, as if he didn't already know the answer.

"The harbour," we shout, "then home by Girdleness."

So along Union Street we go, turning down Market Street, past the station to the harbour. Dad drives slowly along Regent Quay and Waterloo Quay towards Hall Russell's shipyard. We wind down the car window to see the ships, reading out their names and where they've come from. There are ships from Norway and Finland bringing timber, and from Russia with its unreadable script. There's the St Clair, smoke pouring out of its funnel, getting ready for the overnight sail to Shetland.

We trundle our way along the quayside, past cranes and lorries, bumping over the granite setts and tramlines, then turning left towards Torry, climbing the slope overlooking the breakwater at the harbour entrance, up to the lighthouse and foghorn at Girdleness. We stop and watch the light flashing round and round and sometimes, if we're lucky and it's a foggy night, we wait, fingers in our ears, for the foghorn to boom out its sombre warning to the ships at sea.

As the evening light dims, Dad steers the car south along the narrow, twisty back roads, through Cove and Findon. We pass Mr Anderson's farm, Barclayhill, Mr Ritchie's Mains of Findon, and Gavin Duncan's Blackhill. We drive under the railway bridge, down to the Mill, where Marie Henderson, one of the Sunday School teachers, lives with her family. Dad slows the car so that we can watch the swans gliding over the millpond and look to see if the mill wheel is turning. Then it's up the hill to the Mains of Portlethen, swinging right past the church and the school, turning up into the Manse Road and into the courtyard. Home! Mum is there in the warm kitchen, waiting to welcome us, eager to hear all about our big night out.

June

Florence Dunn, Sandra and Marilyn Dunn, Lily Hourston, our cousin, in Portlethen Moss. The radar pylons are visible on the horizon.

Peat Cutting in Portlethen Moss

It's a warm, sunny Saturday morning in June and we're off to start cutting the peat. Up the Manse Road we go, past the wood with its sycamore trees and snowberry bushes, past grassy verges bright with buttercups and daisies and harebells and the white lace caps of cow parsley. Dad leads the way, dressed in his old brown tweed trousers and his Shetland Fairisle jumper, the peat spade, sharpened and gleaming, over his shoulder. Me and Stuart and Marilyn in our dungarees and wellington boots skip along beside him.

We turn left up Glascairn Road, following the drystane dyke till, at the edge of the moss, it gives way to an avenue of gorse, the golden yellow flowers glistening in the sunshine, dark prickly branches standing guard like well-armed soldiers. We walk along the track cocooned in the strong, spicy scent, the air singing with the hum of a thousand bees.

We reach the crossroads. The track on the right winds

through a swaying forest of rosebay willow herb up to the farm at Balquharn, and to the left carves its way through the clumps of yellow broom towards the Walker's house at Mosside. We carry straight on and follow the well-worn footpath through a sea of heather, pink and rose, russet brown and purple, rolling away into the distance. We walk single file, footsteps bouncing over the dry springy turf, past the Milne's peat bank, then down the slope to the low lying, boggy level where peat was dug out long ago. Here the path winds its way over squelchy, spongy sphagnum moss, between tussocks of sharp-leaved cotton grass till we come to an old drainage ditch and cross over on a plank of wood. We turn left and follow the track alongside the brown peaty water till we reach a clump of silver-leaved alders and willows. We pause and peer among the lower branches. They're there! Survived the winter! A little garden of wild orchids, poking their bright pink heads through the tussocks of grass and rushes at the edge of the ditch! Somehow we know without Dad saying a word that these flowers are rare and precious, that we mustn't pick them and we shouldn't tell anyone where to find them.

Then it's on we go again, following the path out of the bog through the heather till we reach our own peat bank. We haven't been here since last autumn so we go on a tour of inspection. Here's the shelter Dad has made by cutting a corner into the bank, with benches carved out of the peat, and a roof of wooden planks covered in turf, to keep us snug and dry if it starts raining. Here's the overhang where we keep the peat barrow with its big front wheel and long wooden handles. Here's the mound of heather where we lie and look up at the sky and know we are hidden and no one can find us.

We hear Dad calling us. It's time to settle down to work. Dad has been busy cutting through the top layer of heather and throwing the turfs down the bank to give him a dry foothold to stand on. Now he uses the right-angled peat spade to slice through the waterlogged bank like a knife through butter and cut blocks of wet, heavy peat. He swings round and slaps the peat against the bar at the front of the barrow. It's cut, slap, cut, slap until the barrow's full. Stuart bends down, grips the handles and trundles over the heather to the flat area where me and Marilyn are standing waiting. We grasp the peat, fingers sinking into the sodden slabs, and plonk them down on the heather, two by two. Stuart waits till we're finished then off he goes back to Dad.

All morning we work, cutting, barrowing, lifting, laying, till the wet dominos of peat file across the heather like well-behaved schoolchildren lining up two by two in the playground. Mid-morning we hear a "Cooee" and there, making their way towards us over the heather, are Mum and little sister Sandra, carrying baskets covered with red checked dishtowels. We stop work and run to meet them and tell them how hard we've been working. We all go and sit on the peat bench in the shelter and Mum pours out cups of hot, sweet milky tea from a flask and hands out newly baked scones, spread with butter and strawberry jam.

I sit munching my scone and look out over the moss, watching the white, fluffy seed heads of the cotton grass dancing in the breeze and listening to a skylark singing high overhead. On the skyline I can see the stone circle at Aquhorthies. I know from school that people in the Bronze Age built it more than three thousand years ago. I wonder if there was a girl my age standing up there in the sunshine all these years ago, looking down on the moss where we are now. How surprised she would be if she knew that the plants she could see, the heather, the alders, the rushes, the sphagnum moss would drink in the light and warmth from the sun then take it down with them into the dark, dank depths and there it would lie hidden till our family years later would dig it up and take it home so that the sunshine from long ago would keep us warm in the dark winter nights.

July

Children waiting in the Manse courtyard for the bus
to take them to the Sunday School picnic.

The Sunday School Picnic

It's the day of the Portlethen Sunday School Picnic and we're packed into two buses on our way to Balmedie Beach. There are about a fifty of us children, along with Mums and Dads, Sunday School teachers and some of the church elders. The sun is shining and we're all fidgeting with excitement. The singing starts as soon as our bus turns onto the Aberdeen road.

There were ten green bottles hanging on the wall, we sing as we bowl along past Hillside and Nigg, down the slope towards Aberdeen. By the time we slow down to cross the Bridge of Dee we're in full voice:

There were fleas, fleas
With kilts and hairy knees
In the quartermaster's store.

Up the hill we go towards Hilton then down towards the Bridge of Don, swinging north on the Peterhead Road to the sound of *She'll be coming round the mountain when she comes.*

We drive past the Gordon Highlanders' barracks and then along the road till we reach Balmedie. I can see Dad up the front of the bus telling the driver this is where we turn off and down the narrow track we crawl till we reach the car park. We tumble out of the bus, clutching sand pails and spades, footballs and cricket bats. George Main, my Sunday School teacher, marshals us into line.

"Follow me," he says and off we troop along the path through the sand dunes. Mum and Dad and the other grown-ups bring up the rear carrying bags and boxes full of food and drink, rugs to sit on and towels to dry our feet.

"Ouch!" says Frannie Middleton as the marram grass scratches her bare legs.

"I've got sand in my shoes," says little sister Sandra.

"So have I," comes back a chorus of voices.

We wind our way along the path, up and down over the sand dunes, till at last we crest a hill and there below us we see miles and miles of empty sandy beach and the sea stretching to the horizon.

We kick off our shoes and socks as fast as we can, and run bare-footed down the slope of the dunes, slipping, sliding in the loose sand, out across the beach, racing helter skelter over the tideline littered with shells and driftwood, down for a paddle in the sea. We girls tuck our dresses into the elastic of our knicker legs and shout and laugh as we jump over the waves, shrieking as the ice-cold breakers chase us up the beach. My brother, Stuart and some of the older lads wade out on to a sand bank till Dad comes and shouts at them to come back or they'll get marooned when the tide comes in. Sandra and Frannie are making a sandcastle, decorating it with shells and bits of seaweed. Marilyn and I go to help them, digging a moat and a channel to the sea to let the water flood in.

Mum has spread a green tartan rug on the slope of the dunes and is sitting chatting to Miss Richmond – she's the church organist but also teaches the infants in the Sunday School. Mum has a cardigan draped round her shoulders. The sun is shining but there's a chilly wind blowing in from the sea. I know Mum is keeping an eye on us all to make sure we're safe.

" Time for the races," shouts Dad, and we all run to gather round him.

"Miss Richmond's class first," he says and the little children line up.

"Now when I drop my hanky I want you all to run as fast as you can. Do you see where Mr Milne and Mr Sim are holding the rope? Right, one two three, go."

Dad drops his hanky and off runs Sandra and Frannie and their little friends.

"Come on, Sandra," shouts Marilyn but it doesn't really matter if she wins or loses because everyone gets a three-penny piece at the end.

Then it's Marilyn's turn. She's running a three-legged race with Jacqui Wright. They hang on to each other, arms round the waist, and run as fast as they can up to the rope. My race is an egg and spoon race, except we don't have eggs, just potatoes. Me and my friend, Kathleen, keep dropping our potatoes which slows us down. I'm sure some of the others are secretly using their thumb to hold their potato because they don't drop theirs once. Impossible! Still we all collect our threepenny piece, so we're quite happy. We run back to the start to cheer on Stuart and Sandy Milne. They're in the wheelbarrow race with Stuart trying to go as fast as he can on his hands while Sandy holds onto his legs. They're useless, keep collapsing in hoots of laughter, come in last.

"Right, all you ladies," shouts Dad, "It's time for the Mothers' Race."

We make a beeline for our Mum and try to coax her to take part, but no luck. She shakes her head, and says no, that she's too old, too slow, and too shy. We give up. But then it's the Fathers' Race and we know Dad's not too shy. He loves the chance to run. When he was younger he played rugby for Glasgow University. He's tall and long-legged and he can run like the wind. He comes first by a mile and we're so proud of him.

The races are over and now it's time for the picnic. We sit down on the sand and the Mums come round with egg sandwiches, bags of crisps and a paper cup full of lemonade. We're hungry and so it doesn't take long for the food to disappear. Then while the grown-ups clear away the picnic, we have time for a slide among the dunes, a run along the sand and a last paddle in the sea.

After a while, the call comes,

"Time to go home," and we sit down to rub the sand from between our toes, pull on our socks, lace up our shoes and follow Dad through the dunes, back to the buses.

The singing starts the moment we leave. This time it's:

We're no awa tae bide awa

We're no awa tae leave ye

We're no awa tae bide awa

We'll aye come back and see ye.

We sing all the way home.

August

Jimmy Nicol presenting the prize for Dux of Portlethen
Primary School to Marilyn Dunn in June 1956

Sale of Work

It's almost time for the Sale of Work to start. I'm standing behind my stall with my friends, Kathleen Milne and Elsie Main. We're in charge of the sweet stall and we've got trays and trays of tablet and treacle toffee and fudge set out on the table along with little packets of sweets, jelly beans, fruit gums, peppermints and toffees. On the bench seat behind the stall we've a pile of brown paper bags and a tin box for the money. We're fidgeting with excitement – can't wait to start being shopkeepers.

The Jubilee Hall is crammed with people, old folk and children, mums and dads carrying babies and toddlers. I can see people from Portlethen and the farms round about, but I know others have come on foot, on bikes and in cars from Findon and Downies and Newtonhill. There's a buzz of anticipation as I watch Dad climb the steps on to the platform followed by Jimmy Nicol who's going to open the Sale of

Work this year. The crowd in the hall hush as Dad, in his dark suit and dog collar, holds up his hand and starts to speak.

"Ladies and Gentlemen, I want to welcome you all here today to the Portlethen Church Sale of Work, and have great pleasure in introducing our guest of honour, Jimmy Nicol. Most of you know him as the farmer at Clashfarquar, but you may not be aware that he's well known all over the world as a breeder and a judge of Aberdeen Angus cattle. We're grateful that he's found time in his busy life to be with us today and I invite him to say a few words."

We all clap and look at Jimmy Nicol, a small man with a grey moustache in a tweed suit, and listen as he starts speaking in a gruff, Aberdeenshire accent, telling us how pleased he is to be here and hoping we'll enjoy ourselves and give generously because all the money raised today will go to support Portlethen Church. He finishes, "I declare this Sale of Work open."

Then we're off and for the next hour it's non-stop, serving customers, wrapping up toffee, working out prices, taking the money, giving change. We smile at the old folk, wait patiently for the little children to make up their mind what to buy. At last there's a lull and Elsie says, "Elizabeth, do you want to go and have a look round? Kathleen and I will manage."

"I'll be back in a wee while," I say, grabbing my shoulder bag with my purse full of pocket money. I set off to explore.

First stop is my sister, Marilyn's stall. She's on "Bunty Pull the String." There's a board with a hole in it and lots of strings hanging down. I watched Marilyn and her friend, Jacqui Wright, last night spend ages tying strings to pencils, notebooks, toy cars, lollipops and all sorts of little bits and pieces. I pay sixpence, choose a string and am now the proud owner of a biro pen. Very useful!

I move on down the side of the hall, set out with card tables covered in white tablecloths. Mrs Blacklaw and her staff of waitresses are pouring cups of tea and serving scones and jam. I poke my head into the kitchen behind the platform and see Mrs Milne presiding over the tea urn. It's all a bit frantic, so I quickly retreat.

Next, I visit Mum's stall in front of the platform. She's on the Craft Stall along with Mabel Coutts and Miss Richmond – lots of knitted matinee jackets and tea cosies, home sewn aprons and peg bags. Mum smiles but she's too busy to talk.

I move on to the Produce Stall, bright and colourful and full of lovely smells. There are baskets of strawberries and blackcurrants, gooseberries and apples, cartons of eggs, crates of lettuce and carrots and potatoes, jam jars filled with lilac sweet peas and crimson roses. There's even a box of crabs donated by the local fishermen – lots of customers are queuing up, so it looks like they'll soon be sold out.

I turn round and bump into my little sister, Sandra. She's wearing a flowery summer dress but on top is a yellow zip-up jacket with the Famous Five logo. I know Mum sent away for it for her and has tied a matching yellow ribbon in her brown, bobbed hair. She looks pretty as a picture and she's holding a beautiful doll wrapped in cellophane paper tied with a pink bow. I give her sixpence and watch as she puts it carefully in her shoulder bag. I choose a birthday for the doll and write my name in the diary she's carrying. If I've chosen the correct birthday, I'll win the doll. I'm a bit too old for dolls but I could always give it to Sandra.

At the next stall I find my brother, Stuart, presiding over the bran tub. There's a huddle of young girls queuing up to chat and the chance to plunge their arms deep into the tub of sawdust and come up with a mystery parcel. I can see Stuart is doing a roaring trade – not surprising. I've heard Stuart's teachers saying to Mum and Dad that what he lacked in hard work and effort he more than made up for in good manners and charm. I wonder if his charm will help him earn his living when he grows up?

I make my way outside and join the crowd of people round the swing boats. Last night we watched Dad, Mr Adam, the blacksmith, and some of the other elders carry the wooden planks and beams out of the shed behind the Hall, bolt them all together and pull them upright. Me and Marilyn and Sandra rocked up and down in the half-moon boats as they sat on the ground until the men came to lift them up and attach them to the cross bars. Now I watch as people pull on the ropes, swinging higher and higher, shouting and waving to their friends down below. It looks great fun. I run back into the Hall and ask Elsie, "Can Kathleen come with me so we can have a shot on the swing boats?"

"Off you go," says Elsie, "I'll manage."

So me and Kathleen join the queue, pay our sixpence and clamber aboard our swing boat. We each grab hold of a rope, and then swap them so that we're pulling on crossed ropes. Kathleen's Dad releases the brake and gives us a push to get us started. We pull, first me, then Kathleen, taking turns. Up and up we go, up over the wall till I can see over the fields full of corn, over Portlethen moss with its heather and clumps of trees, up the slope to Boswell's Monument on top of the hill behind Cairnwell. I hear the creak of the ropes and feel the wind blowing my hair and tugging at my dress. I use one hand to tuck my skirt under my legs so I'm not showing my knickers to all the lads in the other boats. I look across at Kathleen and see her freckly face shining with the effort of pulling but we laugh and pull harder, swinging higher and higher. Oh no! I feel the scrape of the brake under the boat. Mr Milne has decided we've had our money's worth and it's time to stop. We keep pulling on the ropes to try to make the ride last a little longer but it's no good. With a grate and a rasp the boat slows to a stop and Mr Milne helps us out.

"That was good fun," we say as we weave our way back through the crowds to tell Elsie and let her go to have a turn. We go back to playing shopkeeper till all the sweets are sold. We clear away the crumbs and labels and bags and trays from the stall and carry the moneybox through into the kitchen and give it to Mr Sim for counting.

The Sale of Work is drawing to a close. I watch people gather up their bags and their children and begin to make their way out of the Hall. I see a little girl hugging the doll in its cellophane wrapper with the pink bow. I'll need to ask Sandra what was its correct birthday. Obviously it was not the 10th May which was my guess.

Me and Kathleen go outside and stand and watch Mr Milne and the other men, with a bit of help from Stuart and Sandy Milne, dismantle the swing boats and carry them back into the shed behind the Hall. It's sad to think we won't see them again for another year.

We wander back inside and go to find Kathleen's mum. She's in the kitchen helping with the counting of the money. We watch as boxes are brought in from the stalls, tipped out onto the table and the notes and coins separated. Mrs Milne and some of the other ladies pick out the half crowns and set them in piles of eight alongside piles of ten florins and twenty shillings. We ask if we can count the pennies and set them in piles of twelve next to the threepenny pieces and the sixpences. Mr Sim is writing down the totals on a sheet of paper, just like a real banker. Mum and Dad come in to watch. I see Mum taking an envelope from her handbag and handing it to Mr Sim.

"Jimmy Nicol gave me this as he was leaving," she says. "He said it was a donation to our funds. It's a £10 note."

Mr Sim opens the envelope and I see his eyebrows shoot up and his eyes widen behind his glasses.

"It's not a £10 note," he says. "It's a £100 note."

Mum gasps and looks like she needs to sit down. Everyone in the kitchen comes crowding around, passing the £100 note from one to the other. I've never seen a £100 note and neither has a lot of other people.

"Good old Jimmy Nicol," says Mr Sim, and I hear lots of other people saying what a nice man he is, so generous.

Dad is smiling and looking very pleased and I know he is thinking that it's been a good Sale of Work, lots of hard work, lots of fun and raised lots of money for Portlethen Church.

September

Portlethen Manse with the garden, outhouses, courtyard,
Manse Road and Gushetneuk

Bringing Home the Peat

We're up with the sun, me and Marilyn and Sandra, on with our dungarees and down the stairs to the kitchen. Mum is standing at the stove stirring the porridge. Dad, dressed in his old brown cord trousers and his tartan shirt, sprawls in a chair, drinking a cup of tea. Stuart wolfs down a slice of toast and marmalade, laces up his tackety boots and heads for the back door.

" I'm off to Balquharn to get the tractor," he shouts. "See you in the moss, Dad."

We hear the gate clang and see him whizz through the courtyard on his bicycle. Dad finishes his tea and, with a smile and a wave, goes out the back door. We follow him to the gate and stand watching him stride up the Manse Road towards Gushetneuk. Mr Milne and his son, Sandy, are waiting to join him and we see the two men marching along with Sandy trotting behind until the three of them turn up towards Glascairn and disappear among the gorse and the birch trees that mark the edge of the moss.

Then we wait, and wait. We stand on top of the drystane dyke and scan the horizon. We listen. All we hear is the wind rustling the leaves in the beech trees, the twittering of the swallows as they wheel overhead and the cluck of the hens as they scratch around among the nettles. We wait.

At last, we hear the faint chug chug of a tractor on the Aberdeen road, getting louder and louder until it comes into view and turns down into the Manse Road. We watch it swaying, rocking, dragging the cart piled high with peat, snorting clouds of smoke, coming closer and closer till it reaches us, and swings through the back gate into the court-yard. We run to tell Mum but she's heard the sound of the engine and is standing waiting, smiling at the driver, Harry Nicol, the farmer at Balquharn. He reverses the cart up to the stable door, jumps down, and turns the crank handle. Up tips the cart and down rumbles the peat into a big heap. Harry Nicol winds the cart upright, has a quick chat with Mum and sets off back up to the moss.

As the tractor leaves, into the courtyard come Mrs Milne and my friend, Kathleen, from up the road. They've come to help. Now it's all hands on deck. We pile the peat one on top of the other in the crook of our arm, carry them into the old stable and throw them into the stall. Back and fore, lift and carry, bend, straighten. Some of the peat are scratchy and twiggy and hurt our hands. Dust gets in our hair and eyes and makes us cough but we keep going until at last we've cleared the first load. Mum fetches a pot of tea and some scones from the kitchen and we sit on the doorstep of the washhouse to rest before the second load arrives and we start all over again.

All day we work, hot, tired, grey with dust. The stack in the old stable gets higher until we have to build a wall with the peat to keep them in place. We throw the peats up, up over the wall till they almost touch the rafters. As the afternoon sun sinks towards the hills and the tractor delivers another load we hear the words we've been waiting for.

"The next load is the last," says Harry. "Any of you bairns coming?"

"Yes! Yes! Yippee!" we shout.

"Off you go," says Mum. " Elizabeth, look after your sisters."

We clamber into the empty trailer, crouching down on the dusty floor. Mum and Mrs Milne watch and wave as we rumble out of the courtyard. Then we're slowly bouncing along in the ruts and puddles, up the Manse Road. We turn onto the main road and pick up speed, out amongst the cars and buses and lorries, the exhaust from the tractor flying overhead. Then it's slow again as we turn in through the gate into the field, bumping over the stubble, creeping carefully over the wooden planks that bridge the ditch and into the moss. We follow the track through the heather and gorse and there's Dad and Stuart, Mr Milne and Sandy, beaming and waving, standing waiting for us by our peat bank.

We jump down and everyone starts scooping up the last of the peat, throwing them into the cart. Finally, we're finished.

"Right, up you go," says Dad and lifts us one at a time onto the trailer. I make myself a level seat on top of the stack and pull Sandra close to make sure she's safe. Marilyn and Kathleen sit close by. Stuart and Sandy find a perch on the hub of the tractor wheel, hanging onto the back of the driving seat. Dad is having a last blether with Harry and Mr Milne, thanking them for their help in bringing home the peat, and so from my high perch I've time to look around.

I can see the purple of the heather stretching away to the edge of the moss and now and then a clump of birch or alder. I can see lots of white fluffy cotton grass dancing in the wind and the tall stalks of reed surrounding the dark brown pools in the old peat banks. Up the brae beyond the edge of the moss, I can see the farms: Balquharn where we get our milk, Cairnwell where we go to pick brambles, Whitebruntland where my friend, Hazel Mann, lives and Clashfarquar with its black Aberdeen Angus cattle. I can see the spindly legs of the radar pylons at the RAF station and next to them the shadowy outline of the stone circle at Craighead. I can see the kirk on top of the hill where Dad preaches on Sunday and beyond it the cold grey North Sea where we go to paddle and look for gulls' nests.

I'm jolted out of my daydream as with a puff and a snort we're off, creeping along the track, through the prickly yellow gorse, over the planks, out of the moss, through the field and up onto the main road. Now we're flying and I hold onto my sisters to keep them safe. We see people in cars pointing at us and waving. We laugh and wave back. Then it's slowing to turn into the Manse Road, a last sway and bounce through the puddles and we're home.

Mum is waiting in the courtyard, glad to see her chickens back home safe and sound. She thanks Mrs Milne and

Kathleen for their help and we say cheerio as they leave to go and make tea for their family. We start lifting and carrying and soon Dad and Stuart join us and as daylight fades we work to bring the last load of peat into its winter home. In the twilight we stand together in the stable and look at the stack.

"Do you think we have enough to last the winter?" asks Mum.

"Yes," says Dad, smiling.

The gales can howl in from the North Sea, the icy wind and snow can blow down from the Grampians but this winter there will be warm peat fires in the Portlethen Manse.

October

Arial photograph of Portlethen taken in September, 1954,
showing the farms and fields, roads and railway line,
Portlethen Moss and the radar pylons.

Tattie Picking

Time to get up, children," shouts Mum from the foot of the stairs.

I crawl out of bed in the cold, grey dawn of an October morning, rubbing my eyes and thinking, "Why am I having to get up so early? Oh yes, I remember. It's the tattie holidays. I've got to go to work."

So it's on with the jumper and dungarees and downstairs for breakfast. Stuart and Marilyn are there in the warm kitchen, quiet and sleepy eyed. We tuck into a bowl of porridge and milk, then it's on with our wellington boots and out to the garage to fetch the bikes.

We cycle down the Manse Road, round the corner past the Post Office and the school, over the railway bridge, past Dad's church, and down the hill to the Mains of Portlethen. We can see a huddle of grey-coated figures in the field that slopes down to the sea, dump the bikes by the roadside and climb over the drystane dyke to join them. I say hello to my friend, Kathleen. Most of the other children I recognise from school.

As we wait, into the field puffs the big green Case tractor, dragging the potato digger, Mr Shand at the wheel. We're used to seeing Mr Shand in the church but today he's not dressed in his dark suit and tie. Today he's the farmer, our boss, wearing a brown tweed jacket and a flat cap, looks very stern, a bit scary. Next comes another tractor, pulling a cart piled high with metal baskets, driven by Eddie Shand, with his fair, curly hair. Some of the girls think he's quite good looking but I prefer Sandy Shand – he's always smiling and joking. He's walking along beside the cart, lifting the baskets – we call them sculls – and throwing them down alongside the potato drill.

"Aye aye, Elizabeth," he says as he passes, "Foos you?"

"Fine, Sandy," I reply, half shy, half pleased he's noticed me.

Next comes Rob Shand, the oldest brother, very business-like, marching into the field with an armload of stakes and a hammer. He strides over to the start of the potato drill and starts pacing, counting out loud – one, two, three. When he reaches twenty-five paces, he stops and hammers in a post.

"Stuart, that's your bit," he says.

Off he goes again, pacing, counting, pegging, calling out a name. Eventually, I hear, "Elizabeth, this is your bit," and I go to stand at my post. Marilyn is on one side of me, Kathleen on the other. That's good. We can help each other out and I know that both of them will work to their peg and not cheat by doing less or, worse still, moving the peg. We all get paid the same so we all should pick the same amount of potatoes.

Finally, when we're all ready, there's a snort and a cloud of smoke and off goes Mr Shand and his digger, whirring and clattering as it sends earth and stones and potatoes flying. We wait till the tractor passes, grab a metal scull and then it's head down, legs astride, fingers flying, picking up the potatoes, throwing them into the scull, dragging it forwards, working till it's full, dumping it to one side, fetching another. Ten yards left. Keep going. At last, finished. Look up. How's Marilyn doing? Does she need help? No, she's finished as well. Where's the digger? Making it's way round the field back to the start of the next drill. There's time for a rest.

I find an empty scull, turn it upside down and sit on it. I look out over the field, down to the grey North Sea and watch a fishing boat sailing by, heading for Aberdeen. I hear the distant crash of waves against the cliffs and the call of the seagulls round May Craig, just off Portlethen shore, remembering the fun we've had there, paddling and clambering over rocks, and fishing in pools.

Time to stop daydreaming. Here comes the digger. Start again. Bend, pick, lift, drag. Back starting to ache. Leg muscles sore. Hands cold and filthy. Dirt under my fingernails. Wellington boots heavy with mud sticking to the soles. Keep going, row after row.

At last, there's a shout, "Piece time."

I look up and there's Mrs Shand coming into the field carrying a tea urn, and Eileen Shand with a basket over her arm. The digger stops and we all troop down to the gate where Mrs Shand is dishing out mugs of hot sweet tea and baps filled with strawberry jam. Time to catch up with friends.

"How're you doing, Kathleen?"

"Fine," she answers, "but I wish that tractor would go a bit slower."

"I wish that tattie howker would break down," mutters her brother, Sandy, looking over his shoulder to make sure none of the Shands are listening.

I'm hungry and tuck into my bap, teeth crunching on the crystallised sugar in the jam. I cup my hands round my mug of tea to warm them. I watch Mr Shand and it's not long before I see him finishing his tea and handing his cup back to his wife. I bet he's thinking, "Time is money. I'm not paying these kids to sit around gossiping. There's work to be done."

He strides over to his tractor and starts up the engine. There's a chorus of groans and boos as, reluctantly, we finish our tea and trudge back to our posts. Off we go again, row after row, hour after hour, picking the potatoes, filling the sculls, bending and stretching, lifting and carrying. There's a stop for lunch and then it's back to work for the afternoon. A cold wind is blowing in from the sea bringing the salty, seaweed tang to mingle with the musty stench of wet earth and rotting vegetation. Oh no, it's starting to drizzle with rain. My hair is soaked and cold drips are running down the back of my neck. I'm wet, sore, muddy and miserable. I hate the sight of potatoes. I hate Mr Shand and his digger. I wish I was home, curled up in front of a warm fire with a good book. But it's head down, keep going.

As the afternoon wears on, the sun sinks behind the hills beyond Netherley and the daylight fades. At last, it's lousing time and a cheer goes up as we watch the tractor and digger leave the field for the day. We pick our last potato, stand up and stretch, arching our backs to ease the pain. We clamber wearily over the dyke, get on our bikes and cycle home.

Mum is there in the kitchen with little sister, Sandra. There's a hot bath waiting and a change of clothes and soon we're sitting down at the kitchen table, tucking into a big steak pie. Mum listens to our moans and groans, then reminds us that on Friday it'll all be worthwhile because we'll get paid. We can buy new bikes, or books, or anything we like. Yes, the work is hard, but if we can grit our teeth and put up with it, there'll be a reward at the end.

November

John Mearns who used to bring his concert party
to Portlethen Jubilee Hall

The Concert

There's a buzz of excitement in Portlethen Jubilee Hall as we wait for the concert to start. I'm sitting on a bench in the second row with my sister, Marilyn, on one side and my friend, Kathleen, on the other. Brother Stuart is in the row behind with his pals and little sister, Sandra, is sitting on Mum's knee in one of the rows behind that along with all the other Mums and Dads, grannies and grandpas. The Hall is packed with local people, all looking forward to a great evening's entertainment. They know Johnny Mearns from his radio programme and lots of them have already been to one of his concerts. I've heard Dad say that he started his concert party during the war to raise money for the Red Cross and to cheer people up when everyone was scunnered with bombing and rationing and worrying about Hitler and the Germans coming ashore on Aberdeen beach. I know he takes his concert party to other village halls but tonight we're lucky and he's here in Portlethen.

After a while, the lights in the hall dim, the door at the side of the stage opens and up the steps and onto the platform comes a lady in a tartan skirt. She sits down at the piano. Next comes a man in a check shirt carrying an accordion. He sits down on a chair. He's followed by a dark haired man who sits down behind the drums and picks up the sticks. They give us a smile, and then strike up a tune, a foot-tapping, hand-clapping reel. Just as they finish, the door from backstage opens and up onto the platform comes Johnny Mearns. Such a cheer goes up from the folk in the Hall it's a wonder the roof doesn't fly off over the fields and into the North Sea. He's dressed in tartan trousers and a tweed jacket, a tam-o'shanter on his head and a tartan plaid over his shoulder. I think he looks a bit like one of the local farmers and he certainly speaks just like them with words we use in the playground, but know not to use in the classroom.

After a bit of blether and saying how pleased he is to be back in Portlethen, he launches into his first song, "The Barnyards o' Delgaty," in a voice that bounces off the walls and can be heard right to the back row. It's the story of a working lad going to the market in Turriff to find himself a job as a ploughman and ending up on a farm with an "auld grey mare sat on her hunkers" and another horse that "wadna rise at yokin' time." We all know the words of the chorus and join in with:

> Linten adie toorin adie
> Linten adie toorin ae.

There's cheers and claps at the end, and then, when there's a hush, Johnny tells us stories about himself growing up on his father's farm in Fintray and makes us laugh. After that he sings again, "The Old Meal Mill," a slow, lilting song about a young farm worker who stables the horses for the night then runs through the heather to meet his lass down by the Mill.

And so the concert goes on with a mix of stories and poems and Bothy Ballads – songs written by ploughmen and cattlemen, working and living together in bothies on farms scattered over North East Scotland, full of characters that seem familiar and places we know. There's jolly songs like "Aikey Brae," serious songs like "The Work of the Weavers" and gentle love songs like "Lassie wi' the Yellow Coatie." We hum along to the tunes, and rock from side to side with the rhythm. We tap our feet and clap our hands and sing our hearts out in the chorus.

At last it's my favourite, "The Bonnie Lass o' Fyvie," which tells the story of a troop of Irish Dragoons who came marching into the village of Fyvie and the Captain who fell in love with a girl called Peggy. We join in the chorus:

Now there's mony a bonnie lass in the Howe o' Auchterless
There's mony a bonnie lass in the Garrioch O'
There's mony a bonnie Jean in the toon o' Aberdeen
But the flower o' them a' is in Fyvie O'.

The words of the song tell us that the Captain had to follow his colonel's orders and march off, leaving his bonnie lass behind, and pined so dreadfully that he fell sick and died. It's such a sad story I feel like crying, and have to swallow hard to get rid of the lump in my throat. Fortunately the next song is "Granny's Old Armchair" which is a bit cheerier and we're back laughing again and Johnny Mearns is saying, "Fit a grand nicht we're a' haen."

And it feels like he enjoys being here with us, and he can see that all of us who live in Portlethen with its scattered houses and farms and fishing villages are loving him and his music, that we've left our worries outside and we're here in our village hall laughing and singing together and enjoying ourselves.

In the blink of an eye, it's time for Johnny Mearns to sing his last song, "Hame and Guid Nicht," and to bid us all farewell and promise to come back next year. We clap and cheer and stamp our feet, then tumble out of the Hall saying,

"Wasn't that a grand concert?"

We find Dad outside, buttoning up his overcoat against the cold night air, and Mum holding Sandra by the hand. Dad has a torch and lights the road home in the darkness. Mum tucks her hand into the crook of his arm and we hop and skip along beside them with the words and the tunes singing in our ears and the kindness and good cheer warm in our hearts.

December

Children in Class 1 and 2 in Portlethen Primary School, 1948

The Christmas Tree

It's Christmas Eve and we are standing at the dining room window in the Manse watching and waiting for our Christmas tree to arrive.

"Can you see them?" asks Sandra, standing on her tiptoes to peer over the windowsill.

"Not yet," says Stuart.

"I think I can hear something," says Marilyn. I listen but all I can hear is the faint rustle of dried leaves in the beech hedge and a robin singing in the ash tree.

We wait. We've been waiting since the beginning of December for our Christmas tree. We've watched coloured lights appear in windows all over Portlethen and on Friday nights, when Dad drives us into Aberdeen for our music lessons, we've counted the number of Christmas trees we see in houses all along Holburn Street and Albyn Place. We're always the last to get a tree because our tree has places to go and things to do before it comes to the Manse.

Every year someone in the parish of Banchory Devenick cuts down one of the big fir trees growing in its forests and donates it to the parish of Portlethen because we don't have any forests. A man in a truck drives it to the Jubilee Hall and Dad and the elders carry it in, set it up on the platform and decorate it with lights in time for the Sunday School Christmas Party.

I like the Christmas Party. Me and Marilyn and Sandra put on our best dresses and Mum battles with Stuart to try and get him to wear his kilt. The party always starts with The Grand Old Duke of York. Eileen Milne plays the piano and me and my friend, Kathleen, link hands and gallop up and down the hall, then form an arch for everyone to skip under. Next comes "The Farmer's in the Dell" and I hope that I'll get picked early to be the farmer's wife. I hate when I'm picked to be the "bone" because everyone shouts, "The bone won't break" and thumps you on the back and which is really uncomfortable. We play "Pass the Parcel" and "Musical Chairs" and sing the "Hokey-Cokey" until it's time for something to eat. We sit on benches round the side of the hall and Mum and some of the other ladies from the Women's Guild come round with plates of sandwiches and glasses of lemonade. Then there's jelly and ice cream, which is a real treat. Dad collects the ice cream from town in the morning in a metal can, which smokes with dried ice when he lifts off the lid.

Afterwards we run around the hall while the plates and cups are cleared away. Then someone turns out all the lights except those on the Christmas tree and Dad announces that Santa Claus is coming. There is a murmur of excitement and the door behind the stage opens and in comes Santa Claus, except I know it is really Mr Sim dressed up because we all watched Dad fetch the Santa outfit from the attic this morning and check to see everything was in the box. There was a bit of a last minute panic because he couldn't find the beard and Mum had to quickly make one by gluing cotton wool onto some white paper.

Santa is carrying two big sacks full of parcels, one for the girls and one for the boys. The other children think the presents come from the North Pole but we know they come from The Rubber Shop in George Street in Aberdeen because we went there yesterday with Dad to collect them. The shop assistants choose them from their toy department and wrap them up ready for Dad to collect. Now he reads out the names of children in the Sunday School and we all go up one at a time, shake hands with Santa and get a present from the sack. Everyone rushes back to their seat, rips off the wrapping paper and "oohs" and "aahs" about their presents till there's such a racket that Dad has to shout out the names of the last few children.

Then the party's over and everyone goes home except us. We wait while Mum and the other ladies clear up in the kitchen. I pop my head round the door and see Mr Sim struggling out of his Santa outfit and hear him complaining to Mum that he almost passed out with the fumes from the glue on the beard. In the meantime Dad and the elders strip the lights off the Christmas tree, tip it on its side and carry it out through the hall door. It's getting dark outside now and we stand at the gate and watch the torchlight procession make its way along the road past the school and the shop, over the railway bridge and up the hill to the church.

The next morning it's the Christmas Service at church. We dress in our Sunday best coats and hats, file into the Manse pew with Mum and look around. There next to the communion table is the Christmas tree standing tall with its bright lights shining amidst the sunlight dancing through the stained glass window. I can see that Bodge Murray, the electrician, has been helping his father decorate the church because chains of coloured bulbs trace the outline of the pulpit and festoon the pillars in front of the choir stalls. It looks so pretty.

The service starts with "O come all ye faithful" and "Hark the herald angels sing" and then Dad reads the story from the Bible about the shepherds and the three wise men. We sing "O little town of Bethlehem" and I think of what it was like for Mary trying to keep her baby warm and safe in that stable so long ago. We finish with "Away in a manger" and then Dad comes down from the pulpit and walks with his head bowed along the aisle to the door of the church where he stands shaking hands and wishing everyone a Merry Christmas. We walk home with Mum and the Milnes from up the road but Dad stays behind to wait for the Christmas tree.

So now we are standing at the window in the Manse, eagerly watching for signs of activity. At last we hear a crunch of feet on the gravel path, a creak of the front gate and there they are, Dad at the head leading the way, Mr Milne carrying the middle section of the tree and Mr Adam at the back. We rush to open the front door and in they squeeze, the branches scraping along the coat stand sending a patter of pine needles onto the linoleum. Mum watches nervously as they manoeuvre in through the drawing room door and set the tree upright in the bay window.

"It's too big," says Mum. "It's touching the ceiling."

So Dad sends Stuart to fetch the saw from the garage, tips the tree on its side, spreads some papers to catch the sawdust and cuts off a slice from the trunk. The men set the tree upright again and this time it doesn't quite touch the ceiling. Mum is pleased and goes off to the kitchen to cook the Sunday dinner. Dad leaves the room to show Mr Milne and Mr Adam out and thank them for helping carry the tree down to the Manse.

We stay with the tree, gently touching the branches, stroking the sharp needles, rubbing our fingers over the rough trunk. We breath in the smell of resin as we welcome this visitor from the wild pine forest to our home this Christmas.

Dad comes back and sits down on the floor.

"Right, pass me the box with the lights," he says. I hand him the cardboard box that we've brought downstairs from the attic.

"I wonder if they're all still working," he says.

He carefully lifts the first set out, untangles the wires and lays it out on the floor. He pushes the plug into the wall socket and switches it on. Nothing happens.

"Hmmm. Pass me the box of spare bulbs, Stuart."

We all sit quietly, patiently, cross-legged on the carpet and watch as Dad unscrews the first bulb, replaces it with a new one. Still nothing. He replaces the original and tries the next bulb, and the next till finally the set of lights burst into a chain of bright colours. We clap and cheer. Now for the next set of lights. Again there's a problem and Dad has to methodically test each one till he finds the "dud" and replaces it. Finally all the bulbs are working and we watch Dad stand on a kitchen chair and carefully drape the lights over the top of the tree, round and round, down and down, till every branch shines with a star of light.

Now at last it's our turn. We start with the decorations from the box in the attic. We lift out some old green glass baubles that belonged to our grandparents and hang them very carefully near the top of the tree. We hook silver foil candles and crystal glass icicles over the branches and drape them with sparkling silver tinsel. Then we add our homemade decorations, paper chains and lanterns painstakingly cut from gummed coloured paper. Mum comes through from the kitchen to tell us that dinner is ready.

"That's beautiful," she says and we watch the lanterns twirling and the tinsel sparkling among the coloured lights and think, yes, it is beautiful.

On Christmas Eve we sit round the peat fire and talk about hanging up stockings and presents we might get, and the lights from the Christmas tree shine out from the Manse window over the fields and farms of Portlethen.

Postscript

Our family left Portlethen in 1966 when my father retired but I have returned frequently over the years and have watched Portlethen being transformed from a village to a town, seen the ruts and puddles in the Manse Road disappear under tarmac, and the expanse of Portlethen Moss and the surrounding fields shrink under houses and supermarkets. I have been amazed to see the station reopen, the construction of a Library, an Academy, a Sports Centre. How different it is for children growing up in Portlethen now! Yet amidst all the changes our old home, The Manse, still stands tall among the new buildings, the Church still stands on top of the hill, the skylarks still sing over the heather and gorse in Portlethen Moss and the seagulls still call from the cliffs along the shore.